SCANNING
FOR
SIGNAL

Copyright © 2016
All rights reserved.

This book or part thereof may not be reproduced in any form, stored in a retrieval system, or transmitted in any form by any means-electronic, mechanical, photocopy, recording, or otherwise without prior written permission of the publisher, except as provided by United States of America copyright law.

The information provided in this book is designed to provide helpful information on the subjects discussed. This book is not meant to be used, nor should it be used, to diagnose or treat any medical condition. The authors and publisher are not responsible for any specific health needs that may require medical supervision and are not liable for any damages or negative consequences from any treatment, action, application, or preparation, to any person reading or following the information in this book.

References are provided for information purposes only and do not constitute endorsement of any websites or other sources. In the event you use any of the information in this book for yourself, the author and the publisher assume no responsibility for your actions.

Books may be purchased through booksellers or by contacting Sacred Stories Publishing.

SCANNING FOR SIGNAL

Kaitlin Abendroth
Kiah Abendroth
Patricia Brooks
Evan Corey

Tradepaper ISBN: 978-1-945026-21-8
Electronic ISBN: 978-1-945026-22-5

Library of Congress Control Number: 2016950937

Editor: Evan J. Corey
Cover Photography: Kaitlin Abendroth
Cover Design and Interior Images: Mikaela San Pietro
Published by Sacred Stories Publishing, LLC
Delray Beach, FL
www.sacredstoriespublishing.com

Printed in the United States of America

SCANNING FOR SIGNAL

KAITLIN ABENDROTH
KIAH ABENDROTH
PATRICIA BROOKS
EVAN COREY

This is a book for those who have never had the space to simply *be*.

TABLE OF CONTENTS

It seems loneliness... 3
Stop coming close... 5
Our story began in the Winter... 7
I think I'd fit in more in space... 9
There is a feeling of you... 11
Now I lay upon the floor... 13
Sadness... 15
I don't know why... 17
The less you say... 19
I mostly reserve my conviction for fiction... 21
Madness... 23
You shout your words at me... 25
I speak so many words... 27
I feel you... 29
We both knew the script by heart... 31
Today... 33
What a delight it would be... 35
My inferno stomach... 37
It's not that I never wanted to be here... 39

Who is the voice in my head... 43
I'm walking through a dark forest... 45
It could do us all well to learn... 47
They aren't us... 49
And then... 51
Break me... 53
The rain sings to me... 55
The traits not celebrated... 57
When I step into judgment... 59
My body shatters... 61
You cast me aside... 63
Let me be Seen... 65
Maybe the flower... 67
I worry that the world is becoming... 69
I wonder if... 71
So many hearts... 73
Can I touch you... 75
What if we choose to... 77
If I fall in love... 79
It's you and me... 81
I want my sun... 83
Sweet... 85
I sat on the park bench... 87
I wonder if I could stop being afraid today... 89
Voices speak to me of change... 91
There is nothing but silence... 93
I look up far... 95
Moonlight calls to me... 97

Oh empty shell of my broken spirit... 101
Never fear the unknown... 103
It is in the darkness... 105
Opportunity can't knock... 107
A person faces two battles in life... 109
The stars shine brightly... 111
Sometimes a lesson that needs to be learned... 113
When the path is winding... 115
Of all the things that Life is... 117
Sometimes a smile... 119
As we arrive in our place of Need... 121
As my side is brushed... 123
I want to know my soul... 125
Broken on the ground ...127
Let me be all the colors of the rainbow... 129
Flowers are miraculous beings... 131
They said she would never bloom... 133
You are a beautiful soul... 135
In movement we are reaching... 137
Where is your inner Light... 139
In seeking to find myself... 141
Every thread... 145
You are loved and you are worthy... 147
Wait for the day... 149
I pray for... 151
Let me be free... 155
I dipped my toes... 157
I just wanted to say thank you... 159

PROLOGUE

There is another Me.

I know it.

I feel it.

For seeds planted in snow

Have nothing to grasp

No way to grow

Dear God, The Universe, Source, Whoever You Are:

Would you help me?
I don't know where I'm going.
My heart is reaching out, the broken pieces of me
Falling down like dust.
Can you help me?

There is no way to find you in all of this darkness…

It seems loneliness
Waits more patiently
Than friendships do.

I know it would be easier for both of us
If I could befriend loneliness,
But loneliness
Just doesn't like me like that.

Stop coming close,
With your sharp words,
And those jagged thoughts.

Please,
Keep to yourself.

Can't you see
They cut into me?

Our story began in the Winter,
And there it all ends.
For seeds planted in snow
Have nothing to grasp
No way to grow.

I dream of your
Soft soil eyes
Sprawled amongst the daisies
Of sweet splendid
Springtime.

But the sun came and went
Before we were ready.
The leaves dried
And fell.
And all fell with them.

I think I'd fit in more in space.
If I could step out of the gravity of this situation,

Would you slip away with me?

There is a feeling of you
I can't shake.

Ingrained
In my bruised brain.

I sift through your soul
Like sand
In an hourglass.

Tick tick
Tock tock

Don't break.

Now I lay upon the floor.
Can someone come and
Clean up the pieces?

What about when no one is home?
Will I lay forever abandoned between the cracks of the floor?

Swish, swish…
Whoosh, whish…

There I go again.

Scattered.

Sadness
Courses through the cells of my body.
A heaviness weighs me down.

Everything is an effort,
Even the smile I put on my face
So others won't notice.

I don't know why
Babies cry
Clouds drift
Tears fall
Peace is elusive
Time passes
Hearts break

The less you say
The more they'll listen
When you do speak.

The trouble is
Remembering how
At that point.

I mostly reserve my conviction for fiction.
Imagine that.

Madness.

In silence
It screams out,
All those pieces of your soul
You've so sanely
Kept hidden.

You shout your words at me,
Loud claps of thunder across a stormy sky.
They startle and frighten me.

You say I don't listen,
But you don't speak in a way that
I can hear.

My mind is closed to you now,
Your assault too great.

I speak so many words
But the truth is unheard.
The depths of that ocean
Lie within me,
Hidden from the eyes of the world.

I feel you
Pounding on my chest
Trying to get out.

Boom boom.
Boom boom.

I just can't let you go.
I don't know how.
I don't know if I want to.

We both knew the script by heart.
Our disagreements unending.
Two performers in a play
Forever acting out our roles.
Performance after performance,
In a drama that should have long closed.

Today,
I am tired.
I am tired of my goals,
Of my plans,
Of believing,
Of trusting,
Of trying so damn hard.

What a delight it would be
To turn yourself off.
Physically.
Entirely by definition.

Imagine an off switch,
Right at the base of your neck.
You switch it down and you

Turn.
Off.

Like a child's toy.
Like the last light in a restaurant
Moments before the door is shut,
The lock is turned.

You are unneeded at this point in time.
Please cease to exist, indefinitely.

To be inanimate for a while.
What a delight that would be.

My inferno stomach
Heats my stone heart and
Boils my veins.

My head is steam and smoke.
My feet,
Glowing embers.

He calls for me to
Grow.

An innocent request
From a soft soul
Who has never played with fire.

It's not that I never wanted to be here.

I just never asked.

And now I have all this stuff to do.
And you never told me how.

Relief and loneliness at the same time

There is a beauty to the certainty

Who is the voice in my head?

There are times I think I know.
Times that I feel it is a beautiful, powerful guide
Who's loving and affirming words I can take refuge in.

And then there are times I do not know.
Times I feel no connection.
Times I think it is me.
Times I want it to stop talking.

I'm walking through a dark forest.
I'm chasing after someone.
A girl.

She radiates with warmth and light,
Beauty and joy.

I look nothing like her.
My body is colorless and pale.
My dark lifeless hair clings to my back, wet.

Then I see her.
I race forward, groping desperately for her arm,
But my hand hits something hard instead.
In front of me, battered and worn, is a mirror.

I spin around, assuming she is behind me,
But no one is there.
I am alone.
I always have been.
Alone in this forest of mirrors.

It could do us all well to learn
That not all silences
Are empty things
That need to be
Filled.

They aren't us.

They don't see through our eyes
Or touch with our hands.

They don't feel the quickening of our hearts
Or the catch of our breath.

They don't wonder of our future
Or cry our endless tears.

They don't know.
They aren't us.

And then,

Sometimes,

There is only me.

Relief and loneliness at the same time.

There is a beauty to the certainty.

Break me.

Help me.

Set me into freedom,

Into motion.

Stop me.

Still me.

Help me be free

From my pendulum

Of

Thoughts

And

Words.

Keep me.

Hold me.

Don't let me fade away.

The rain sings to me
A soft melody,
Again and again.

It lulls me into a place
Where all my thoughts
Can lay their weary heads.

It unravels my heart
One fragile thread
At a time.

The traits not celebrated
Were the ones I clung to.

I believed

They were all
I had to offer.

When I step into judgment of myself
Do I diminish the Divine Light that I am?

For how can I shine my own Light bright
While casting a shadow of judgment within?

My body shatters,
Glass falling,
Slowly,
Breaking into a thousand pieces.

I lay on the asphalt,
Glittering
In my new
Brokenness.

People walk over me.
Through me.
Some carry me with them,
Dust on their moving feet.

The sun shines through me,
Dancing in circles in my being.

Maybe it's not so bad,
Being broken.

You cast me aside,
A useless shell.

You were too narrow-sighted
To see the seed fall
From that cast-away debris,

To notice me take root
Amongst the brush,

To watch as I grew
And found my inner glory
Shining out.

Let me be Seen.

Not in a way that's
Pleasing.

But in a way that's
Honest,
Free,
Radiant.

Maybe the flower
Dreamed of flying.

That's why,
Day by day,
It reached its arms up
And into the sky.

I worry that the world is becoming

Less specific.

Less unique.

Blurred together in an age

Of conformity,

Filled with

Whatevers

And

I Don't Cares.

I wonder if
My words can affect,
My arms can hold,
My tears can release,
My Spirit can take,
The pain in this world?

So many hearts
Locked away
In our time.

Password protected.

Perhaps the rare seekers
Should get a tattoo
Of a WiFi symbol.

Just so we know
Who is open
For connection
And scanning for signal.

Can I touch you?
Touch your hand?
Touch your mind?
Touch your heart?
Touch your senses?
Touch your soul?

What if we choose to

Be the Light
In another's darkness?

Hold space
For another's pain?

Be a balm
On another's wound?

Be comfortable
In our uncomfortableness

For Another?

If I fall in love
Will you dive in and save me?

I've waded in before,
Just ankle deep.

Enough to see
Love
Is much too wild
To find one's way
Alone.

It's you and me,
My ghosts set free.
We flee the heartache

Together.

I want my sun
To warm the soil of your soul
And help you grow.

But my light filters through the trees
And can only dapple the ground on a clear day.

If only you were a meadow.
But you are not.

Still, I will shine for you,
If only to warm your leaves.

I must accept that, perhaps,
You don't want me to reach your piece of earth.
And perhaps I am not meant to.

Sweet
Are the days
That are soft and gentle.

Vibrant
Are the days
That are full of love.

Brilliant
Are the days
Of conquering dreams
And fears.

Perfect
Is the day
When I am set free.

When all days
Become
One.

I sat on the park bench
And listened to the whispers of the trees.

The rustling of a thousand parts
Roaring into one.
A symphony of soft silken leaves
Swaying in the crisp breeze,
Chattering of years long past
And days to come.

Stories untold to the likes of me.
But I still listened,
Always almost understanding.

I wonder if I could stop being afraid today.
I can be smart,
But I don't need to be afraid.

Fear will not prepare me,
The wolves will come if they come.

But fear is the only thing
That will actually eat me alive.

Voices speak to me of change.
Sometimes in silent looks,
Or with shaken faces
and teary eyes.

Not one of us has been built to know it all.

So we stand on the edge
Looking into both darkness and light,
Beauty and mystery,
Wanting to jump into it and
Wondering why we might choose to dance
With such a wild
And concealed
Thing.

There is nothing but silence
All around my spirit.
It whispers to me
From its unspoken life.

"Come closer…"
"Come closer…"

I lean into it,
Longing.

I look up far
Up to the stars
So far that time
Can't quite catch up.

And even if they've long died out
Their essence dances with us
All the same.

Moonlight calls to me,
Building a path on the sea.
"Just one step," she says.

Darkness surrounds me,
The embrace of peaceful night.
"Here I am," it says.

The warm Earth holds me,
Whether he wants to or not.
"Don't let go," I beg.

There is nowhere you have been

That has not been worth going.

Oh empty shell of my broken spirit,
Come again to me.
Let me hold you and kiss
Your withered skin.

There is nowhere you have been
That has not been worth going.
With courage you have ventured
To the very heart of yourself.

Now you can know
That even the struggle
Was not a mistake.

It was those moments that
Broke you open.
It was those motions
That set you free.

Never fear the unknown,
For it has answers for you
That you may not have considered.

It is in the darkness,
When our eyes are closed,
That we heal.

Do not fear the darkness
For it comes with rejuvenation.
It comes to aid the light.

Opportunity can't knock
If you haven't built a door.
Build one on the wall,
The ceiling
Or the floor!

For no matter how loudly you yell,
"Come in!"

Opportunity can't come to you
Without a place to begin.

A person faces two battles in life.
One with their inner fears and demons,
And one with everybody else's.

The stars shine brightly.
They are easy to appreciate.

But don't dismiss
The space in between them,
For that is something truly magical
And full of possibilities.

Sometimes a lesson that needs to be learned
Can look so much like
The world trying to tear you apart.

When the path is winding,
Rocky and steep,
Let me dance with my fleeting feet.

When the trail is calm,
Smooth and bright,
Let me look to the Sky
And share in its Light.

For with every step
I find my way,
Even when I've gone astray.

There is no place
From which I part
With my own precious and lively heart.

Of all the things that Life is,
It is most definitely
Art.

Sometimes a smile
Given to the silence
Echoes louder
Than any words at your disposal
Ever could have.

As we arrive in our place of Need,
Comfort has already been Awakened in the
Heart of Creation.

We may stand, at the edge,
And look out for Answers.

And far away, beyond where we can see,
They've already been sent.

Sent to you
On tiny clouds and
Parachutes,
On the backs of bumble bees and
Dragonflies.

They're
On their way.

As my side is brushed
By those I pass,
I feel the pain
Of a thorn
Long forgotten.

I grab hold of it, and
Slowly,
Gently,
Help it out.

The pain was
My friend.

The passersby
My silent saviors.

I want to know my soul.

I want to feel my connection with the birds,
To live in the sunrise and sunset of each new day.

I want to break open with emotion,
For love to permeate every fiber of my being.

I want to fully express the ache in my chest
And the lump in my throat.

I want the salt from my tears
To clear the mist that shrouds my ability to see.

I want to breathe the air of my ancestors
And be in communion with all that is.

I want to remember.
I want to know my soul.

Broken on the ground
The tiny stem lies.
Many people pass without seeing.
Some pass who see, but don't stop.

Then I come down the street.
I bend down and whisper a tiny prayer.

"I know you don't need our love,
But I love you.
Thank you for being here,
For being the life that you are."

For a moment I think of moving it aside.
But it seems to have chosen that spot,
So I leave it there,
Half crumpled into the sidewalk.

As I walk away,
I wonder how many times
I have been passed by
When I lay broken in my chosen spot.

And when,
Even without my knowing,
Someone has seen me
And knelt down in Love.

Let me be all the colors of the rainbow;
All the colors that ever imagined themselves in the sky.

Let me be all of the songs that have been sung, and
All of the silent ones that couldn't find their way out.

Let me bask in the brightness of the day,
And glow with the splendor of the night.

Let me raise my heart to Heaven,
And bask in sheer Delight.

Flowers are miraculous beings.

They live to grow and bloom to the sun.
They brighten the world
Just by living.

I don't think humans
Are too different from flowers at all.

I think we just need to accept
Our own miraculousness.
And let ourselves

Be.

They said she would never bloom.

They were wrong.

You are a beautiful soul
With a place in the universe,
A purpose to fulfill,
Wisdom to share.

In movement we are reaching,
"I am here! I am here!"
Yet it is in stillness that we discover,
"I am here."

The funny thing is,
In an infinite expanse,
Seven billion people
Can each truly be
The Center of the Universe.

Where is your inner Light?
Your inner tree?
Your inner magic?

Speak not to yourself,
But to the Life that lives all around you.

There is magic in the branches,
There is Light in your Soul.

In seeking to find myself,
I first had to lose myself.
For the Me I was seeking
Did not exist.

Now, arms wide open,
I see that I am all around.
That I am more than myself.
That I am limitless.

I am the stars shining brightly
And the moon rising softly.
The wind whipping harshly
And the sea under the sky.

I am you and all the creatures,
I am everything
And I.

There is a joy in me
That rises free
Every time I watch things change.

A smile that comes
Despite the way the winds
May ruffle my feathers.

Every thread
Is woven
Through my heart
And through yours.

Be mindful
What strings you pull.

For what you think is yours,
Is ours.

You are loved and you are worthy.

Not for what you are,
Or for who you are,
But simply because

You are.

Wait for the day
You are so happy that
You see everything in sparkling gold.
You see your purpose for existence
In every flashing of your sight.

Then live that beautiful day,
Every day,
For the rest of your beautiful life.

I pray for

One human species.

One planet.

No boundaries.

Where kindness matters.

Where an abundance of love and peace exists

For all.

Dance softly.
Speak truly.
Live fully.
Break
Wide
Open.

Let me be free
To dance in the sea
With garments of sunlight
Draped around me!

I dipped my toes
In the Universal river today.

I stumbled out of bed and into the current.
The force of the energy and information
Rushed past me and almost
Took me off my feet.

But once I found my footing
I realized I was a part of it.
A ripple in the flow.

Not an obstacle for the swirling droplets,
But an ornament
Decorating the water's passage.

I reached down and cupped a handful,
Watching the light sparkle
As I let it trickle back down through my fingers.

I just wanted to say thank you
For saying
What I couldn't.
For doing
What I wouldn't.
For seeing
What I was blinding myself with
And taking it away from me.

Thank you.
I am fresh.
Once again,
I am new.
And all of this
Is thanks to you.

Dear Sweet One:

There is a way to find me.
I am already holding you.
This darkness is my arms.
The rhythm of your heart, my love.
I can help you,
Always,
When you call.

So gently
Lay yourself down.
The ground is my caress.
Rest here, in my arms,
For now and forever.

Love,

God, The Universe, Source, Whoever You Need Me To Be

EPILOGUE

There's nothing you have lost. Never, ever, have you lost a thing.

In this sweetness that we know as Life, there is only one place and that place holds everything that has ever been and will ever be. We dance between the worlds, free as we are. Do not fear your freedom. In this dance, you will find great Joy, immense Power, and endless Love.

YOUR FELLOW SEEKERS

Kaitlin Abendroth truly found that one of the most wondrous and unique parts of being a human is all of our abilities to create and inspire each other in so many different ways. She has a degree in the Performing Arts and is always searching for new ways to express and discover a little more about herself and what it means to be alive. She would like to thank every single person who has come into her life with love and lessons, as you all have been an endless inspiration. kaitlinabendroth.com

Rev. Kiah Abendroth is an Interfaith Minister and professional trumpet player. She aspires to spread love, connection, and awareness through all she does. It is her sincere hope that the spiritual journey co-created as this book may uplift you and bring you even greater peace and inner-joy. revkiah.com

Evan Corey currently works as an editor as he completes his degree in Communications and Media. He feels most connected when nature surrounds him, and most free when lost in the words on a page.

Rev. Patricia Brooks is an ordained interfaith, interspiritual minister and a sacred storyteller. Patricia believes it is time to raise the vibration of our planet to one of respect and honor for the sacred nature of ourselves and all living beings. The sharing of our hearts and wisdom is a powerful beginning. revpatriciabrooks.com

~The image to the left of the prose indicates the author.

www.ingramcontent.com/pod-product-compliance
Lightning Source LLC
Chambersburg PA
CBHW021148080526
44588CB00008B/265